W9-ARU-223

"I'M NOT GOOD AT FUTURE PLANNING. I DON'T PLAN AT ALL. I DON'T KNOW WHAT I'M DOING TOMORROW. I DON'T HAVE A DAY PLANNER AND I DON'T HAVE A DIARY. I COMPLETELY LIVE IN THE NOW, NOT IN THE PAST, NOT IN THE FUTURE."

## HEATH LEDGER

1979–2008

**ABDO**
Publishing Company

# HEATH LEDGER

## TALENTED ACTOR

BY STEPHANIE WATSON

# CREDITS

Published by ABDO Publishing Company, 8000 West 78th Street, Edina, Minnesota 55439. Copyright © 2010 by Abdo Consulting Group, Inc. International copyrights reserved in all countries. No part of this book may be reproduced in any form without written permission from the publisher. The Essential Library™ is a trademark and logo of ABDO Publishing Company.

Printed in the United States of America, North Mankato, Minnesota
092009
102009

Editor: Melissa Johnson
Copy Editor: Paula Lewis
Interior Design and Production: Becky Daum
Cover Design: Becky Daum

**Library of Congress Cataloging-in-Publication Data**
Watson, Stephanie.
  Heath Ledger : talented actor / Stephanie Watson.
      p. cm. — (Lives cut short)
  Includes bibliographical references.
  ISBN 978-1-60453-789-5
  1. Ledger, Heath, 1979-2008—Juvenile literature. 2. Motion picture actors and actresses—Australia—Biography—Juvenile literature. I. Title.
  PN3018.L43W37 2010
  791.43'028092—dc22
  [B]
                                    2009034353

# TABLE OF CONTENTS

Slade Media Center

# 1

# THE PRICE OF FAME

*H*eath Ledger was just 21 when he finished filming *A Knight's Tale* in August 2000. The movie tells the story of an English peasant, William Thatcher, who poses as a knight to win jousting tournaments. Despite Ledger's young age, he had already acted in two major Hollywood films: *10 Things I Hate About You* with Julia Stiles and *The Patriot* with Mel Gibson. But *A Knight's Tale* was his first starring role.

Filming *A Knight's Tale* in Prague, Czech Republic, was exciting for the young actor.

▸ In 2000, Heath Ledger's career was taking off.

6

▲ LEDGER'S IMAGE AS IT APPEARED ON THE MOVIE POSTER
FOR *A KNIGHT'S TALE*

He had the opportunity to sing, dance, ride
horses, and joust. But when he returned to
Hollywood, the fun ended. Ledger was expected
to get to work promoting the movie. His agent,
Steve Alexander, called him in for a meeting

with top executives from Columbia Pictures, the studio that had produced the movie. When Ledger entered the big boardroom, he saw a table surrounded by marketing executives, all of them wearing suits. Huge posters around the room featured his picture and the slogan "He will rock you."

## THE BREAKDOWN

For the next two hours, the movie executives outlined their plans for Ledger. They were sending him on a world tour through 20 states and 20 countries to promote *A Knight's Tale*. They also had big plans for Ledger's future. They would pay him huge amounts of money to make big-budget, blockbuster Hollywood movies such as *Spider-Man*. "I got this two-hour spiel on how they were turning me into Columbia's new 'It' boy," Ledger recalled.[1]

Many young actors would have jumped at the chance to be molded into a movie star. Ledger was not one of them. He was terrified. "I couldn't speak. I left the boardroom, found a bathroom, shut the door, and just started crying," Ledger said.[2] After a few minutes, his agent came into the bathroom and called his name. Ledger recalled the conversation. "I tell Steve I can't do it, I don't want my life to be in their hands."[3]

Ledger eventually emerged from the bathroom and reluctantly agreed to do part of the promotional tour. Still, the sight of those giant "He will rock you" posters plastered all over Los Angeles filled him with dread.

While the studios attempted to turn Ledger into a star, he wanted to focus on the craft of acting. It was a struggle that would continue throughout his career. The more Hollywood tried to reel Ledger in, the harder he tried to pull away. To escape his growing matinee idol image, Ledger passed over movies he knew would become box office hits. Instead, he took parts in smaller, low-budget films that he knew were risky. Doubts about his talent also hounded Ledger throughout his career. No matter how much praise he received or how many awards he won, he never felt that he was good enough.

"At first, people were trying to shape him as this kind of teenage hunk. And that's so not what he wanted. It was something that he was trying to escape into the world of real artistry."[4]

—*former girlfriend Naomi Watts*

▲ Ledger reluctantly did publicity for *A Knight's Tale.*

## Unfinished Legacy

Ledger's fans, fellow actors, and the media did not share his self-criticisms. They praised his raw talent and loved how naturally he portrayed characters ranging from a tormented ranch hand in *Brokeback Mountain* to a demented super villain in *The Dark Knight*. Despite his reluctance to achieve stardom, Ledger became one of the most successful actors of his generation.

With Ledger's talent and good looks, it was only a matter of time before the media started comparing him to other successful actors. Marlon Brando and Sean Penn were two names that often came up when critics discussed Ledger. These actors also gave a raw honesty to the characters they portrayed. After Ledger's death in January 2008, new comparisons were made—this time to James Dean, River Phoenix, and Montgomery Clift. Just like these

## Just Like James Dean

It is not surprising that Heath Ledger has often been compared to legendary actor James Dean. Both men died young at the peaks of their careers. Dean was 24 years old when he was killed in a 1955 car accident. Ledger was 28 when he died of an accidental drug overdose.

Both actors were extremely handsome, yet they refused to fit the mold of the typical teen idol. Both actors were honored for their work after their deaths. Dean received two Academy Award nominations for *East of Eden* and *Giant*. Ledger won an Oscar for his portrayal of the Joker in *The Dark Knight*.

Though Dean and Ledger were both young when they died, Dean had the shorter career. He starred in just three movies—*Rebel Without a Cause* (1955), *East of Eden* (1955), and *Giant* (1956). As time passed, James Dean became better known for his tragic, early death than for his films.

▲ LEDGER ARRIVED FOR AN APPEARANCE ON *THE LATE SHOW WITH DAVID LETTERMAN* IN 2001.

actors, Ledger died young. And like them, he left behind an unfinished legacy—the promise of a brilliant career that ended far too soon.

# 2

# GROWING UP DOWN UNDER

*H*eathcliff Andrew Ledger was born in Perth, a city along Australia's western coast, on April 4, 1979. Heath spent much of his childhood swimming and surfing along Perth's coast, which is lined with beaches of white sand.

The Ledgers were an unremarkable, middle-class family. Heath's mother, Sally, was a French teacher. His father, Kim, was an engineer and raced cars as a hobby. Heath also had an older sister, Kate. When Heath was ten years old, his parents divorced. Unlike many divorces, theirs

▶ HEATH'S CASTING PHOTO FROM 1995, WHEN HE WAS 16 YEARS OLD

was a friendly separation, and Sally and Kim continued to get along. Heath was able to see the positive side of his parents' breakup. "I had two houses, two sets of rules," he said. "I'd go to one place and when I was sick of that and needed a break I'd go to the other."[1]

Both of Heath's parents remarried—his mother to Roger Bell and his father to Emma Brown. They each had a daughter, giving Heath two half-sisters, Ashleigh Bell, born in 1989, and Olivia Ledger, born in 1997. Heath joked that constantly being surrounded by females helped him learn patience. In truth, his mother and sisters were a very important part of his life. He eventually got a tattoo on his wrist of the letters "KAOS," which stood for Kate, Ashleigh, Olivia, and Sally.

## SCHOOL DAYS

Heath attended Guildford Grammar School, an independent school located along the Swan River about nine miles (14 km) from the city of Perth. The school was nearly 100 years old. Girls and boys can enter Guildford in kindergarten and remain there

### Heath's Name

Heath is short for Heathcliff. His mother, Sally Ledger Bell, was such a fan of Emily Bronte's 1847 novel *Wuthering Heights* that she named her first children after its ill-fated lovers—Heathcliff and Kate, short for Katherine (although the character's name is spelled *Catherine* in the book).

▲ HEATH WITH HIS MOTHER, SALLY BELL, AND SISTER ASHLEIGH BELL, IN 2003

through elementary school. However, after the sixth grade, the classes are only for boys. Heath attended Guildford from elementary school through high school, during the years 1987 to 1996.

In addition to its academic classes, Guildford has a rigorous military cadet program for high schoolers. This program is designed to teach students self-discipline and give them an understanding of the Australian military. It has been in existence since 1904. Students in the cadet program learn skills such as survival, martial arts, firearms, and navigation. Heath knew early on that he had no interest in this military training. "Who wants to shoot an automatic rifle? What was I going to use that for?" he once asked.[2] For Heath, sports offered a way to get out of cadets.

## PLAYING THE FIELD

Before he was a star on the movie screen, Heath was a star on the hockey field. Field hockey is a sport that is similar to soccer except players use a short, curved stick to hit a small ball around the field. Although field hockey is a female-dominated sport in the United States, in Australia it is also popular among boys.

Heath played for his school in local Public Schools Association tournaments, and he was part of the 1990 Kalamunda Field Hockey team's league for children under 13. His father, Kim, was president of the team from 1990 to 1992. Heath later played for his state as well. He was a good enough player that his father thought he might eventually try out for the Olympic men's field hockey team, but Heath had other plans.

## FLAIR FOR THE DRAMATIC

As a child, Heath was glued to the television whenever Gene Kelly movies were shown. Kelly was a U.S. actor, singer, and dancer in the 1940s and 1950s. He helped turn movie musicals into an art form with films such as *Singin' in the Rain* and *An American in Paris*. Heath also liked to sing and act. Dancing was more of a challenge, but he took dance classes to improve his coordination.

Heath was not the only member of the Ledger family with acting aspirations. As a teenager, his sister Kate often performed with local theater companies, including the Globe Shakespeare Company in Perth. Heath often tagged along on auditions. When he was just ten years old, he landed his first acting role as a donkey in a school play. Soon, he got the lead in a local theater company performance of *Peter Pan*. Donning the character's signature green tights was a big leap for the fledgling actor. "It took a lot of guts. For a twelve-year-old kid, that can be damaging amongst your peers," Heath said.[3]

Another risky move was leading his school's dance troupe in the regional Rock Eisteddfod challenge—a dance and performing arts competition that was made up mostly of girls' teams. Heath choreographed an eight-minute dance on the topic of fashion and helped create the sets and costumes. He joked that entering the competition was just a ploy to get out of school and meet girls, but Heath ended up leading his Guildford team to become the first boys' school ever to win Rock Eisteddfod. "I got 60 farm boys who'd never danced before up on stage, and we won!" he recalled proudly.[4]

## FIRST ROLES

Heath was acting in a school performance of Shakespeare's play *Hamlet* when he got his first big break. A local casting agent, Annie Murtagh-Monks, was in the audience. Ledger caught her eye. She saw raw talent in the 15-year-old, but no real ambition to become a famous actor. "He had a natural ability but it wasn't like he was driven to be a star at that age," she said.[5]

By then, Heath's good looks and natural talent had helped him land a few television and film roles, but they were small. Anyone who blinked while watching his first movie may have missed him. His role as an orphan clown

in the 1991 Australian kids'
movie *Clowning Around* was
not even big enough to get
Heath's name in the credits.

Heath also had a small
part in the Australian TV
series *Ship to Shore* in 1993.
The show was about the
adventures of a group of
children living on Circe
Island off the coast of Perth.
He played a minor character
named Cyclist in just two
episodes.

## SWEAT

Murtagh-Monks moved
Heath from little more than
an extra to a featured player
when she got him cast in the 1996 television
show *Sweat* in Australia. The show takes place
at Sports West Academy, a fictional Western
Australian school for gifted athletes.

Heath was offered his choice of two roles—a
swimmer or a cyclist. In another risky decision,
he went for the cyclist part. He knew the part
could be controversial because the character,
Snowy Bowles, was gay. But he wanted to

hone his acting skills and knew this would be a perfect opportunity. The character did get Heath noticed—by both fans and the press.

Unfortunately, *Sweat* was short-lived. It ran for only 26 episodes.

## OFF TO SYDNEY

At just 16, Heath's career was on the right track. He'd already earned one starring role in a television show and several more bit parts. However, he knew he was in the wrong place. Western Australia did not offer enough opportunities for the young actor.

Heath worked to finish his high school exams a year early. He borrowed

---

### Checkmate

Acting was not Heath's only interest. As a child, he liked to swim, snorkel, and surf in the ocean. He raced go-karts and helped his dad fix cars. Heath was also a wizard at chess. He regularly beat his father at the game and almost became a grandmaster—the highest level a chess player can achieve.

Heath's love of chess continued as he grew older, and he claimed to play at least one game a day as an adult. When he lived in Brooklyn, New York, Heath would regularly take part in games with other chess enthusiasts in Washington Square Park.

Shortly before his death, Heath was working on a movie about a chess prodigy. He collaborated with screenwriter Allan Scott to create a film adaptation of Walter Tevis's novel, *The Queen's Gambit*. The project had barely started when Heath died.

After Heath's death, his parents commemorated his love of chess by donating a concrete and marble sculpture of two chessboards to his home city. The sculpture sits along

▲ HEATH, *FRONT ROW ON LEFT*, HAD HIS FIRST FEATURED
ROLE IN THE TELEVISION SERIES *SWEAT*.

gas money from his parents, and with his best
friend, Trevor DiCarlo, drove more than 2,500
miles (4,000 km) across the country to Sydney.
When they arrived, Heath had just 69 cents in his
pocket. But his fortune was about to change.

# 3

# LEDGER GETS NOTICED

ydney had a much larger movie industry than Perth, and it was not long before 17-year-old Heath Ledger landed his first film role. Though it was about teenagers, *Blackrock* was not a typical teen movie. It was a serious—and true— story about a 15-year-old girl who was raped during a party and later murdered. Ledger played surfer Toby Ackland, one of a group of friends who struggle with the seriousness of the crime. It was a small role but it offered a chance for Ledger to show off his developing acting skills.

▶ LEDGER TOOK A ROLE IN THE POPULAR AUSTRALIAN SOAP OPERA *HOME AND AWAY.*

*Blackrock* was released in May 1997. It was a big success in Australia. The movie grossed more than $1 million and was nominated for five Australian Film Institute (AFI) awards.

## MORE ROLES

Audiences outside Australia never had a chance to see *Blackrock* on the screen, but the movie did get Ledger noticed in his own country. It led to several more acting roles, including a part in the children's movie *Paws*. The film was about the search for a hidden $1 million fortune. In the film, Ledger played a student who was portraying the character Oberon in Shakespeare's play *A Midsummer Night's Dream*.

Ledger snagged guest spots in several more Australian television shows, including *Bush Patrol* and the sitcom *Corrigan*. He was also cast in ten episodes of the soap opera *Home and Away*. The show has been a staple on Australian television since the late 1980s. It has launched the careers of many young Australian actors, including Simon Baker, Guy Pearce, and Naomi Watts. Ledger played bad-boy surfer Scott Irwin, who dated one of the show's main characters,

"I'm the worst auditioner, really, really bad. I mean, you're being judged and I'm just so aware of it that it consumes me. I can't relax, I'm tied in knots, so the voice is very taut and tense."[1]

—Heath Ledger

Sally Fletcher. Acting on such a famous and well-established show was a major break for Ledger in Australia, but he was still an unknown to the rest of the world.

## ROAR

Becoming famous in an actor's home country is an achievement, but gaining international fame is the ultimate achievement. That is especially true of starring in a U.S. movie or television show, because the United States has one of the biggest and most recognized entertainment industries in the world. Ledger had his chance to make a name for himself outside Australia when he auditioned for a part in the 1997 U.S. television series *Roar*. The show would be shot in Queensland, Australia, but it was meant to air in the United States on the Fox television network.

Ledger flew to Los Angeles, California, for a screen test in front of studio executives. "The room was packed with suits," he recalled. "After every shot, they swarmed together like a pack of ants on a sweet biscuit, whispering."[2] Though Ledger was jet-lagged, nervous, and younger than the character he was supposed to play, the producer liked his maturity and gave him the part. "It was definitely not my best performance, but something must have gone right," Ledger commented.[3]

The mythical adventure series was set in Ireland in 400 CE. Ledger played Conor, an orphaned Celtic prince who led his people to battle the invading Roman army. Critics hated the series, but some had kind words for Ledger. "As Conor . . . Ledger simply commands the screen," a reviewer wrote in *TV Guide*.[4] Yet despite Ledger's best efforts, only 13 episodes were filmed and only eight aired on television.

Ledger might not have had a hit television show with *Roar*, but

## Missed Opportunity

In the late 1990s, the Fox network was casting for a new show about teens living in Roswell, New Mexico, a city famous for its supposed alien visits. Ledger auditioned for the part of Max Evans, one of several human/alien teens with supernatural powers.

Unfortunately, history was against Ledger. Executives at Fox network remembered him from *Roar*, which had been a flop with both audiences and critics. They did not want to take any chances with another big-budget project on the line. The producers ended up passing over Ledger and casting Jason Behr, who had previously acted on shows such as *7th Heaven* and *Dawson's Creek*.

Ironically, *Roswell* never aired on the Fox network. It was moved to

▲ LEDGER, *CENTER*, DATED HIS FELLOW *ROAR* CAST MEMBER LISA ZANE, *FAR LEFT*.

something good did come out of it. He started dating costar Lisa Zane, who convinced Ledger to come with her to Los Angeles to try to make it big in Hollywood.

## TWO HANDS

When 18-year-old Ledger arrived in California in late 1997, he spent four months meeting with agents. Finally, he was picked up by one of the biggest and most powerful talent agencies in the world—Creative Artists' Agency (CAA). The group has represented A-list celebrities such as Brad Pitt, Kevin Costner, George Clooney, and Oprah Winfrey. Ledger signed on with veteran CAA agent Steve Alexander.

Ledger's first movie role under CAA management was the dark comedy *Two Hands*. In it, he played a tough street kid named Jimmy who gets a job delivering $10,000 for a gangster named Pando. When the money is stolen, Jimmy goes on a race for his life to find the loot.

Ironically, although Ledger had just arrived in the United States, the movie took him straight back to Australia. It was written and directed by Australian Gregor Jordan, who had seen Ledger's performance in *Roar* and wanted to cast the young actor in his movie. Jordan flew to the United States to convince Ledger to take the part. Ledger was thrilled to be working with Jordan and also excited to share the screen with one of his acting idols, Bryan Brown, who played Pando.

*Two Hands* was released in 1999, and it earned mostly good reviews. It also won five Australian Film Institute (AFI) awards. Ledger received a nomination for Best Performance by an Actor in a Leading Role. Though he did not win,

▲ LEDGER WAS NOMINATED FOR AN AWARD FOR HIS ACTING IN *TWO HANDS*.

the acknowledgement helped him gain even more credibility as an actor.

# 4

# HOLLYWOOD
# BOUND

*J*ust two weeks after wrapping production on *Two Hands*, Ledger already had another movie deal in the works. He was called back to the United States to audition for a role in the high school movie *10 Things I Hate About You*. Although it was not as dark in subject as *Blackrock* had been, it was not a typical teen flick.

*10 Things I Hate About You* was loosely based on William Shakespeare's *Taming of the Shrew*. In the original Shakespearean play, a man falls in love with a young woman who is not allowed to

▶ LEDGER LANDED THE LEAD ROLE IN THE POPULAR TEEN COMEDY *10 THINGS I HATE ABOUT YOU.*

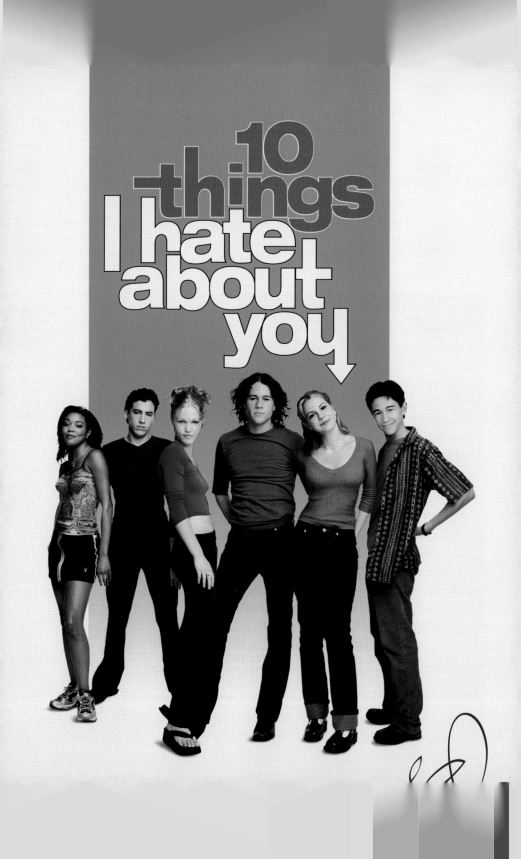

marry until her older sister is wed. The man and his friends use disguises and elaborate schemes to find a husband for the older sister and win the heart of the younger sister. In the movie, a high school student named Cameron yearns to date his pretty, popular classmate Bianca. However, her father has a strict rule that Bianca is not allowed to date until her older, unpopular sister Kat has a boyfriend. So Cameron launches a plot in which he sets up a moody, rebellious student named Patrick Verona to woo Kat. In true Hollywood fashion, the two social outcasts fall in love.

Julia Stiles was cast as Kat and Joseph Gordon-Levitt was the lovesick Cameron. Director Gil Junger

## Singing on the Bleachers

As a child, Ledger had been a big fan of Gene Kelly musicals. Kelly was known for creating dance sequences in unlikely locations, such as on a lamppost in the pouring rain in the 1952 movie *Singin' in the Rain*. In *10 Things I Hate About You*, Ledger had the chance to do his own song-and-dance routine.

Ledger's character, Patrick Verona, takes over the high school's sound system, slides down a pole, and serenades his love interest, Kat, from the bleachers in the middle of her soccer practice. The school's marching band accompanies the song, which ends prematurely when Ledger's character is dragged off by security.

Ledger sings "Can't Take My Eyes Off of You," a song originally made famous by Frankie Valli in the late 1960s. Ledger might not have had the singing ability or experience of a Gene Kelly, but this song-and-dance wanted to find the right actor to play Kat's love interest, Patrick Verona. He had auditioned several actors, but none seemed right. At the last minute, the film's producers convinced him to look at Ledger. Junger knew almost immediately that he had found his Patrick.

As soon as he'd wrapped shooting on *Two Hands,* Ledger flew to Tacoma, Washington, where Stadium High School provided the set for much of the movie. He had little time to rehearse because the production was already under way when he arrived. But he was familiar with *Taming of the Shrew* and had always wanted to act in the play. To capture Patrick, Ledger combined elements of veteran actor Richard Burton's performance in the 1967 film version of *Taming of the Shrew* with the edginess of Jack Nicholson.

*10 Things I Hate About You* was filmed in just eight weeks. Touchstone Pictures released the movie in March 1999. It became a big hit with teen audiences. Ledger earned approximately $100,000 for his role. It was not a lot of money by Hollywood standards, but to Ledger, it seemed like a fortune.

## NOT ANOTHER TEEN MOVIE

With a popular movie under his belt, Ledger was on his way. The trouble was that the studios

▲ LEDGER PRACTICED HIS SINGING AND DANCING SKILLS AS PATRICK VERONA IN *10 THINGS I HATE ABOUT YOU.*

envisioned a different future for Ledger than he saw for himself. They wanted him to become a teen heartthrob, starring in one high school movie after another. That was not the career that Ledger wanted.

Though he could barely make rent, Ledger vowed to remain true to himself as an actor. For a year, he passed up every movie that was offered to him. "I was literally living off ramen noodles and water, because I was sticking to my game," he said.[1] As he explained in a different interview, "I felt like my career was out of my hands. . . . And so to a certain degree, I had to go out and destroy my career somewhat in order to rebuild it."[2] Fortunately for Ledger, his plan worked.

> "When I first worked in the industry, it seemed so unbelievably foreign and surreal. The differences between good and bad people were so extreme. The way some people treated others, or held themselves so falsely high, disgusted me, and I promised myself I'd never become like that."[3]
>
> —*Heath Ledger*

## THE PATRIOT

Waiting for the right role turned out to be a good decision. While he was searching for a deeper script, producers were scouting for a young actor to play Mel Gibson's son in the Revolutionary War drama *The Patriot*. Ledger was called in for an audition.

The movie centers on Gibson's character, Benjamin Martin, a hero of the French and Indian War. As the Revolutionary War begins, Martin refuses to participate in more bloodshed. But when his son Gabriel signs up to fight without his knowledge, Martin is forced into battle to protect his family and his country from British tyranny.

*The Patriot* was a big-budget movie and, potentially, another big career move for Ledger. It was also Ledger's last-ditch effort to make it in

▲ LEDGER RODE HORSES IN BATTLE SCENES IN
*THE PATRIOT.*

Hollywood. He was broke. With his career on the line, Ledger blew the audition. Halfway through his lines, he put down his script. He apologized to the producers for wasting their time and walked out of the room.

For many actors, walking out on an audition would have meant the end of an opportunity. However, the film's producer, Dean Devlin, and director, Roland Emmerich, admired Ledger's honesty, and they saw something special enough in his abbreviated audition to bring him back for a second try. He sailed through the next audition and won the part.

Production began on September 7, 1999. The film was shot at locations throughout South Carolina, including the small community of Rock Hill and the historic city of Charleston. Filming wrapped in December 1999. Released in 2000, *The Patriot* became Ledger's first blockbuster film, taking in $113 million at the box office.

## HE WILL ROCK YOU

Thanks to the success of *10 Things I Hate About You* and *The Patriot*, Ledger was becoming a hot commodity in Hollywood. He was offered his next role without having to audition. Thanks to a recommendation from Sony Pictures executive Amy Pascal, who had helped cast Ledger in *The Patriot,* he landed the role of a peasant named William Thatcher in *A Knight's Tale.*

In this story, Ledger's character poses as the fictitious knight Sir Ulrich von Lichtenstein of Gelderland in order to enter jousting tournaments. The movie was based on English author Geoffrey Chaucer's story of the same name in his book *The Canterbury Tales,* but it was set to a modern rock score. Not only was this Ledger's first starring role in a Hollywood movie, but it was also his highest salary to date—$1 million.

Although the 21-year-old actor was nervous about carrying a $45 million production on

▲ LEDGER WORKING THROUGH A SCENE WITH THE DIRECTOR OF *A KNIGHT'S TALE*, BRIAN HELGELAND

his shoulders, he was also excited about the opportunity to portray a Chaucer character. "I knew I was going to have fun telling the story," he recalled in a television interview. "The story was what I really fell in love with, and the whole fairytale-ness of the movie."[4]

*A Knight's Tale* was filmed in the Czech Republic at Barrandov Studios, one of the oldest and largest film studios in Europe. The director, Brian Helgeland, and crew re-created settings from medieval London and France in the Czech countryside.

The movie was physically demanding for Ledger. He had to ride horseback and joust while wearing hot, heavy armor and keeping a large, unwieldy lance pointed straight ahead. In one scene, Ledger's horse reared up and almost rammed the actor's leg into a post.

*A Knight's Tale* earned $56 million and secured Ledger's place in Hollywood. It also got him noticed in public, especially when he went home to Australia. He was often uncomfortable with the attention:

> *If anything you wish that if one place wasn't to change it would be your hometown, but I was back there recently and they were documenting every meal I had every day! It was in the newspaper that I ate fettuccini on Tuesday; that's front page news in Perth!"[5]*

It was just the beginning of the public fascination with Heath Ledger.

## Putting on an Accent

Ledger is a native Australian, but he has had to use a variety of accents over the years to fit the various characters he's played. The drawls, twangs, and other vocal variations Ledger mastered during his career include the following:

- *The Four Feathers*: Upper-crust British
- *Ned Kelly*: Irish
- *Monster's Ball*: Southern drawl
- *I'm Not There* and *The Dark Knight*: American
- *Brokeback Mountain*: Midwestern American twang

# 5

# Rising Star

is success in *A Knight's Tale* led to many more movie offers for Ledger, including the starring role in the comic book–inspired action film *Spider-Man*. Even though he was offered a lot of money for the role, Ledger turned it down. "I refuse to put on tights and play a superhero," he insisted. "It would have been stealing someone else's dream."[1] That dream ultimately belonged to fellow actor Tobey Maguire, who helped turn the film and its sequels into a multibillion-dollar franchise.

▸ Costar Kate Hudson dancing with Ledger in *The Four Feathers*

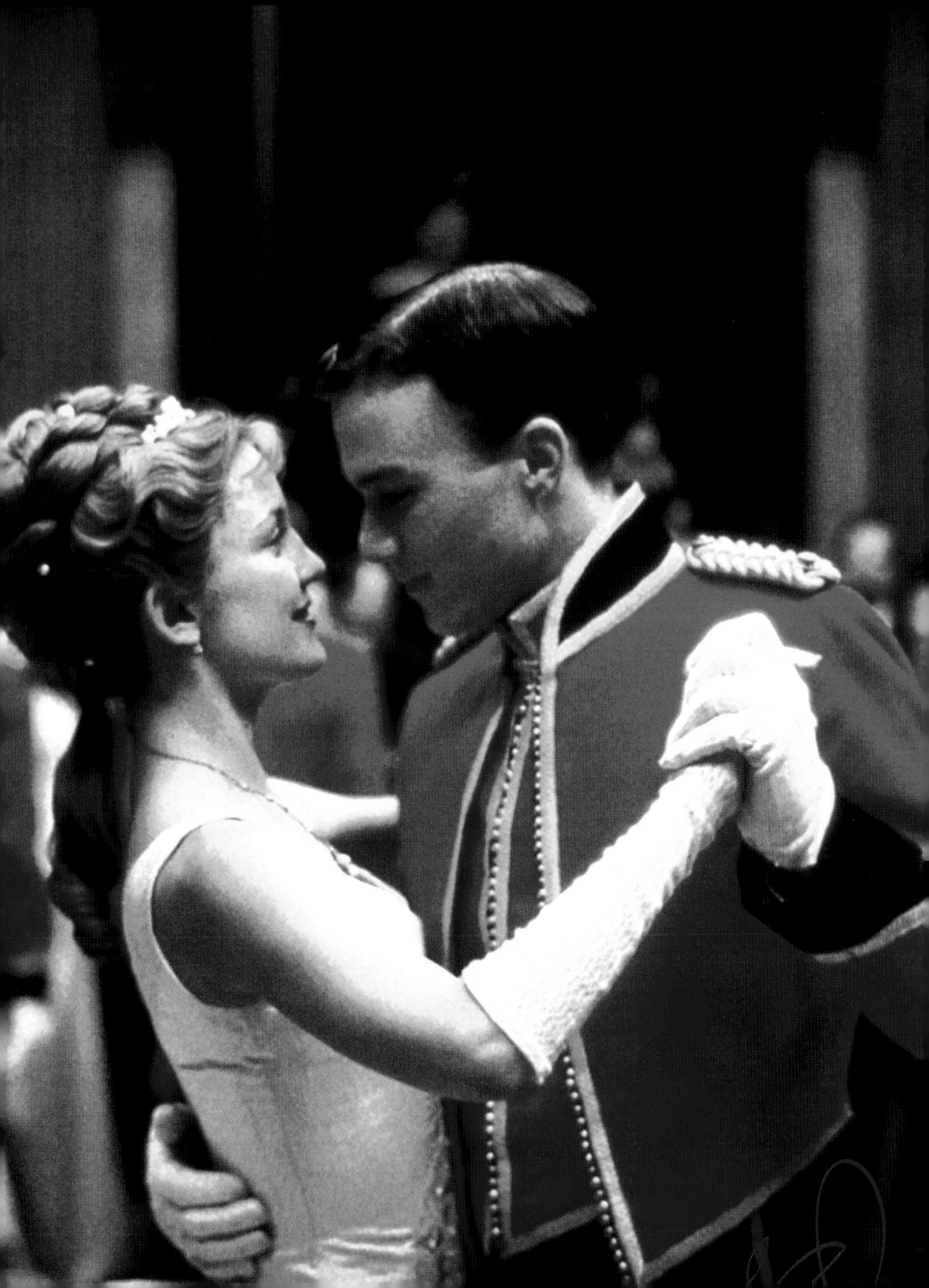

Instead, Ledger opted to try out for a role in *The Four Feathers*, a military adventure based on a 1902 novel by British author A. E. W. Mason. It was the third film version of the story: one movie was released in 1939, and a made-for-television version aired in 1977. After a grueling eight-hour audition in which he had to do a lot of improvisation, Ledger got the part.

*The Four Feathers* tells the story of Harry Faversham, a British soldier who resigns just days before he is supposed to fight in the 1884 Sudanese War in Africa. In response, his three friends and his girlfriend, played by Kate Hudson, each give him one white feather, a symbol of cowardice. Ledger's character decides to go to Africa and fight for his honor.

The movie was filmed in 2001 in Morocco, a country in northwest Africa. It was so hot that many of the cast and crew passed out in the sand. It did not help that the actors had to ride horseback and fight in the heat. Ledger insisted on doing his own stunts, even though many were dangerous. In one scene,

### Old Friends

As Ledger became famous in Hollywood, he stayed true to his old friends in Australia. Because they were not actors, they helped him remember where he had come from and who he really was. In 2001, when *A Knight's Tale* opened, Sony Pictures flew 14 of Ledger's friends from Perth to Los Angeles. Many friends stayed with him at his home.

approximately 100 horses ran toward Ledger. He had to jump onto the back of one of the horses while it was still running and ride away.

*The Four Feathers* was meant to attract a teenage audience. Despite Ledger's appeal to that audience, young people had no interest in the military drama. The movie flopped, earning back only a fraction of its $80 million budget. Ledger did not care. It was not box office returns that he was after. He wanted challenging roles that tested his acting ability.

## MONSTER'S BALL

Ledger found such a role in *Monster's Ball*, the story of a grieving African-American mother, played by Halle Berry, who falls in love with a racist prison guard, played by Billy Bob Thornton. Ledger was cast as Sonny, Thornton's tormented son. After playing the leading man in a few blockbuster films, Ledger enjoyed returning to a smaller part

## Pet Projects

Acting was an essential part of Ledger's life, but it was not his only interest. He also loved music. He and musician Ben Harper cofounded a Los Angeles–based collective of musicians, artists, writers, photographers, and producers called Music Masses. Ledger directed the video for Harper's song "Morning Yearning." He also directed videos for Australian rapper N'fa and singer Grace Woodroofe.

One of Ledger's favorite projects was producing and starring in a music video for a Nick Drake song called "Black Eyed Dog." Drake was a singer-songwriter who had died from a drug overdose in 1974, when he was just 26 years old. His sad story would soon mirror Ledger's own future.

in a smaller movie. *Monster's Ball* was filmed in just four weeks around New Orleans and the Louisiana State Penitentiary. It was a critical success, earning numerous nominations and awards, including a Best Actress Oscar for costar Halle Berry.

## MORE BOX OFFICE DISAPPOINTMENTS

After completing *A Knight's Tale*, director Brian Helgeland was left with fond memories of his young star. He wanted to work with Ledger again when he made *The Order*.

The horror thriller is about a priest, played by Ledger, who travels to Rome, Italy, to investigate a fellow clergyman's death. While there, he discovers that a strange sect called the Sin Eaters is secretly at work within his order.

### Wrong Response

*The Order* was scheduled for release in January 2003, but one big problem delayed it. Often, producers will screen a new movie in front of a test audience before releasing it to make sure viewers like it and react to it as the director intended. During one scene in this dark thriller, audiences had a decidedly different response than was intended. They screamed—but with laughter. The scene used special effects to show sins escaping from people's bodies. What was to have been a terrifying moment in the film was hilarious because the sins looked like giant squid. The director hired a new company to redo the special effects, and the movie's title was changed from *Sin Eaters* to

▲ LEDGER TOOK ON A SMALL BUT CHALLENGING ROLE IN *MONSTER'S BALL*.

Critics' reviews stated that *The Order* was boring and a disappointment; audiences avoided it. It was another box office disaster for Ledger. Frustrated, he returned home to Australia. He reunited with his *Two Hands* director, Gregor Jordan, to film *Ned Kelly*. Though he had reached the $1 million salary mark on his previous films, Ledger was paid only $60,000 to work on *Ned Kelly*.

Ledger played the title character, an outlaw similar to Robin Hood who fought back against the corrupt British colonial system in nineteenth-century Australia. Geoffrey Rush, Orlando Bloom, and Naomi Watts also starred in the film. Ledger was thrilled about getting the part. He had wanted to play Kelly since he was a child. He was so involved in the role that while shooting, he slept in a hotel room overlooking the Old Melbourne Jail, where Kelly was imprisoned and hanged in 1880.

Ledger loved starring in *Ned Kelly*, but once again, audiences were not as impressed, especially those in the United States. The film was released in fewer than 20 theaters and earned only $75,000 in the United States, although it earned more than $6 million internationally.

"The only time that I'm alive and loving and expressing and feeling and relating is when I'm on set during the time between 'action' and 'cut.' That's the only thing that's really important."[2]
—*Heath Ledger*

## LEDGER AND TERRY GILLIAM

Cinematographer Nicola Pecorini was working with Ledger on *The Order* when his colleague, director Terry Gilliam, was casting for *The*

▲ LEDGER SPEAKING TO THE PRESS ABOUT *NED KELLY* WITH COSTAR AND GIRLFRIEND NAOMI WATTS

*Brothers Grimm.* Pecorini recommended Ledger to play one of the brothers. Gilliam's response was, "Heath who?"[3] But once Gilliam met Ledger, he knew he had found the right choice for his film.

Actors often get classified into portraying the same type of character over and over again. Ledger had been cast as the romantic hero in many of his previous roles. Yet in *The Brothers Grimm,* he was cast against type. He played Jacob

▲ LEDGER WORKED WITH COSTAR MATT DAMON, *RIGHT*, AND DIRECTOR TERRY GILLIAM, *LEFT*, IN *THE BROTHERS GRIMM*.

Grimm, the dreamer. Matt Damon was chosen to play the ladies' man, William Grimm.

The pair of actors spent four weeks getting to know one another before shooting began in Prague, Czech Republic. They worked together to develop their characters' personalities and accents

until they had established a
real brotherly camaraderie.

In the film, the Grimm
brothers are con artists who
travel from village to village.
They pretend to remove
mythical monsters (for cash,
of course), until they stumble upon what appears
to be a real-life beast.

"You always know when
you meet somebody who's
going to be a movie star,
because they sparkle."[5]
—*Sony Pictures executive
Amy Pascal*

Although critics mentioned Ledger's abilities,
they were not kind to *The Brothers Grimm.* Roger
Ebert of the *Chicago Sun-Times* said, "Watching
it is a little exhausting," because the film keeps
"chasing itself around the screen without finding
a plot."[4]

Even though it was another unsuccessful
movie for Ledger, one good thing did come out
of it. He formed a tight bond with director Terry
Gilliam. Ledger's last movie role would be in a
Gilliam film.

## LORDS OF DOGTOWN

If Jacob Grimm was a change from Ledger's
usual characters, his next role was an even bigger
departure. In *Lords of Dogtown,* Ledger played
Skip Engblom, a quirky skate and surf shop
owner in 1970s southern California who helps
a gang of skateboarders form into the famous

▲ REFUSING TO BE TYPECAST AS A HANDSOME LEADING MAN, LEDGER TOOK THE ROLE OF A SKATEBOARD SHOP OWNER IN *LORDS OF DOGTOWN*.

Zephyr Team. With his shaggy hair, false teeth, and mumbling voice, Ledger did not look or sound anything like the attractive leading man he often played.

*Lords of Dogtown* was based on a 2002 documentary called *Dogtown and Z-boys,* written by skateboarder Stacy Peralta. Many of Ledger's costars in the movie had been members of the original Zephyr Team. Just as the character he played became a sort of father figure to the skateboarders, Ledger took many of the other actors under his wing. The cast would sit around together and play guitar outside his trailer. It became known as "Camp Heath."

When *Lords of Dogtown* was released in September 2005, critics dismissed the movie and Ledger's performance. It became the latest in a string of disappointments for him. But it would be the last. His next movie was about to break new ground and turn Ledger into a genuine movie star.

# 6

# BROKEBACK MOUNTAIN

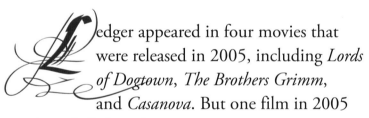edger appeared in four movies that were released in 2005, including *Lords of Dogtown*, *The Brothers Grimm*, and *Casanova*. But one film in 2005 eclipsed all the others.

In 1997, a short story by Annie Proulx about an unexpected but enduring relationship between two Wyoming sheepherders appeared in the *New Yorker* magazine. When screenwriter Diana Ossana read Proulx's story, *Brokeback Mountain*, she convinced her writing partner, Larry McMurtry, to help her turn it into a screenplay.

▶ SEVERAL OTHER ACTORS TURNED DOWN ROLES IN THE CRITICALLY ACCLAIMED *BROKEBACK MOUNTAIN*.

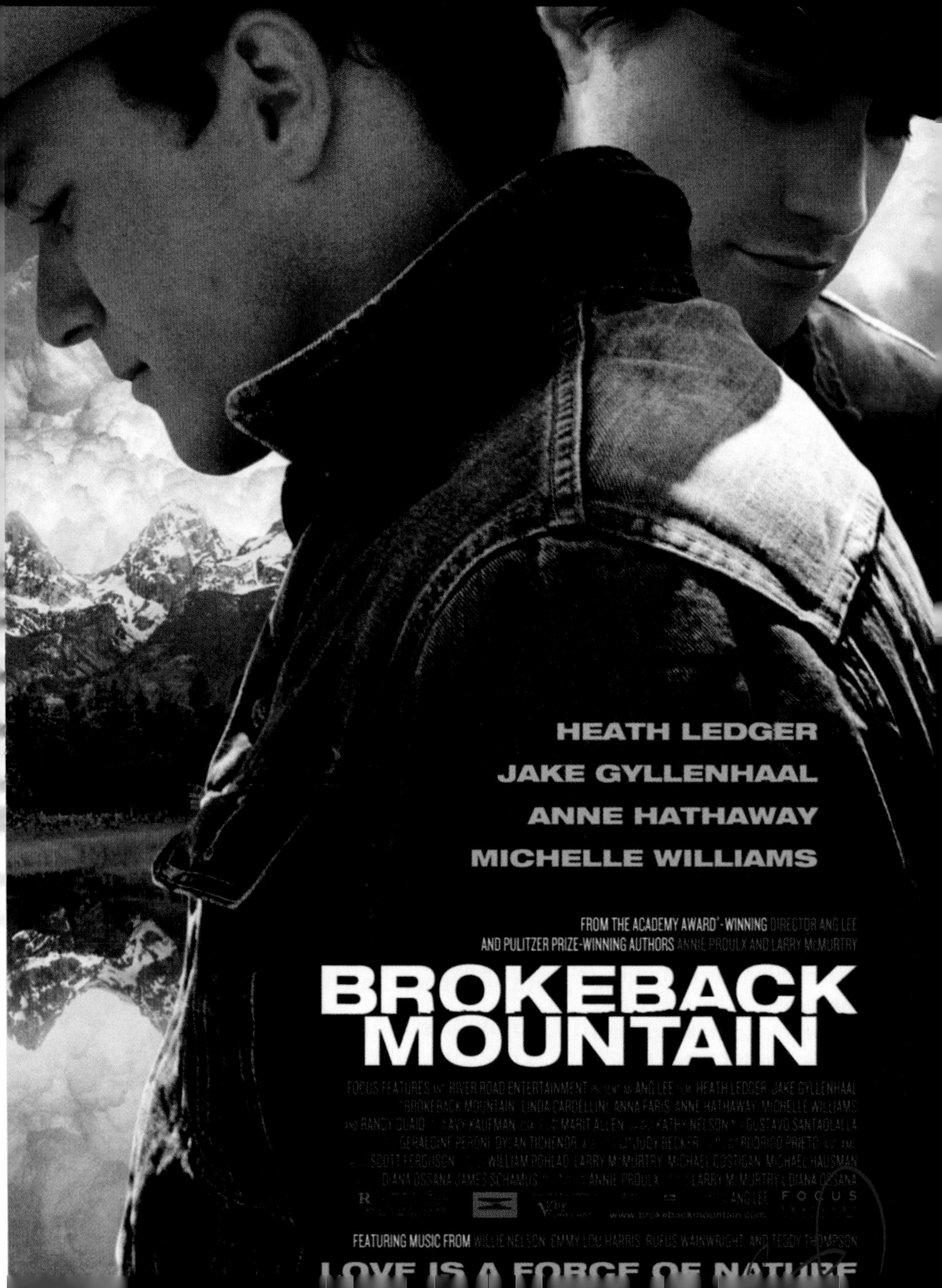
HEATH LEDGER
JAKE GYLLENHAAL
ANNE HATHAWAY
MICHELLE WILLIAMS
FROM THE ACADEMY AWARD®-WINNING DIRECTOR ANG LEE
AND PULITZER PRIZE-WINNING AUTHORS ANNIE PROULX AND LARRY McMURTRY
BROKEBACK MOUNTAIN
FEATURING MUSIC FROM WILLIE NELSON EMMY LOU HARRIS RUFUS WAINWRIGHT AND TEDDY THOMPSON
LOVE IS A FORCE OF NATURE

▲ LEDGER'S POWERFUL PERFORMANCE AS THE QUIET COWBOY ENNIS WON HIM AWARDS AND RAVE REVIEWS.

## RECOGNITION

Ledger earned immediate acclaim for his portrayal of Ennis Del Mar, especially from the story's author. "Heath understood the character better than I did," Proulx said. "It scared me how much he got inside Ennis."[6] Reviewers were also enthusiastic. Peter Travers of *Rolling Stone* magazine wrote, "Ledger's magnificent performance is an acting miracle. He seems to tear it from his insides. Ledger doesn't just know how Ennis moves, speaks and listens; he knows how he breathes."[7]

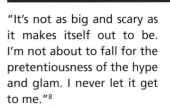

"It's not as big and scary as it makes itself out to be. I'm not about to fall for the pretentiousness of the hype and glam. I never let it get to me."[8]
—Heath Ledger, on Hollywood

Awards season brought more recognition for Ledger and the film. Three of his movies, *Brokeback Mountain, The Brothers Grimm,* and *Casanova*, premiered at the Venice Film Festival, making him one of the most sought-after actors there. *Brokeback Mountain* received dozens of nominations, including eight Oscar nominations, seven Golden Globe nominations, and four Screen Actors Guild nominations. Each of the organizations included a nod for Ledger's acting.

Ledger said that it was an honor to be nominated, but awards were not a big deal to him. Plus, he was not thrilled about the idea of having to do one interview after another to promote *Brokeback Mountain.* "Doing press terrified him, and the campaign was really grueling," said Alexander.[9] Ledger was dating costar Michelle Williams at this time. She became pregnant shortly after they became a couple, and their baby was born just before award season began. The media attention was putting strain on their relationship.

Instead of playing along, Ledger started acting out. His behavior on the awards circuit resulted in Ledger being labeled a "bad boy." When he won the New York Film Critics Circle Award for Best Actor, Ledger did not show up to collect his award. At a Berlin Film Festival news conference, he shocked members of the press by announcing that

## Becoming Ennis

Ledger worked hard to get inside the character of Ennis Del Mar. He tried to adopt many of the characteristics of real cowboys, including their stiff upper lip. "A lot of the ranch hands I've met in Australia, they keep their top lip like that," he said. "I figure it's because they're trying to keep the flies out of their mouth while they're talking." He also picked up the cowboy swagger. "When you're a cowboy, your shoulders and everything slumps when you're on horseback all day. So when you get off, you stay in that shape."[10]

Ledger used his voice to capture the essence of his character. He mumbled many of his lines to give a sense of Ennis's inability to express his true feelings. As Ennis aged in the film, Ledger transformed his voice to mimic the deeper, more gravelly tones of a middle-aged man.

▲ *CASANOVA* PREMIERED AT THE VENICE FILM FESTIVAL IN 2005.

he thought George Clooney should win the Oscar for Best Supporting Actor, rather than his *Brokeback Mountain* costar, Jake Gyllenhaal.

▲ LEDGER APPEARED WITH HIS *BROKEBACK MOUNTAIN* COSTARS, *FROM RIGHT*: ANNE HATHAWAY, MICHELLE WILLIAMS, AND JAKE GYLLENHAAL.

And he delivered a speech at the Screen Actors Guild awards that seemed to mock the idea behind *Brokeback Mountain,* although he later explained that he had been nervous, not disrespectful.

Ultimately, *Brokeback Mountain* won three Academy Awards for Best Director, Best Adapted Screenplay, and Best Original Score. Ledger lost out on the Best Actor Oscar to Philip Seymour Hoffman, star of *Capote.* However, he did win an Australian Film Institute award, a New York Film Critics Circle award, and an MTV Movie Award.

**Heath Ledger's Inspirations**

Most, if not all, actors will say that they were inspired by some of the actors they watched in movies and on television while they were growing up. Ledger's acting heroes included Gene Kelly, Judy Garland, Katharine Hepburn, Jack Nicholson, Mel Gibson, and Meryl Streep.

# 7

# FALLING IN LOVE

*I*t is not difficult for a well-known actor to find romance, especially one as handsome as Heath Ledger. He had a string of relationships with beautiful women throughout his career. One of his earliest relationships was with his *Roar* costar, U.S. actress Lisa Zane. Although the relationship only lasted a short while, Zane was responsible for bringing Ledger to Hollywood.

In 2000 and 2001, Ledger had an on-again, off-again relationship with Australian model Christina Cauchi. While they were together,

▶ LEDGER DATED ACTRESS HEATHER GRAHAM FOR NINE MONTHS IN 2000 AND 2001.

the pair appeared to be blissfully happy. That romance was put on hold when Ledger met actress Heather Graham in October 2000, but the nine-month relationship appeared to be nothing more than a fling.

## NAOMI WATTS

Ledger became more serious when he met fellow Australian actress Naomi Watts in 2002 on the set of the movie *Ned Kelly*. Watts was not familiar with Ledger's movies when they started working together, but his acting amazed her. "It was just something deep in his eyes. You could look into them, and they would tell a thousand stories in one glance," she said.[1] By November of that year, the press was reporting that the couple had moved into Ledger's new Hollywood home and were planning to marry.

Eventually, their ten-year age difference seemed to catch up with them. Watts, who was in her early thirties, reportedly wanted children. Ledger was only in his twenties and was not yet ready to be a father. In May 2004, the couple broke up, but they remained close friends.

## LEDGER FINDS HIS SOUL MATE

When shooting began on *Brokeback Mountain* in 2004, Ledger likely had no idea how much of

▲ LEDGER WITH GIRLFRIEND NAOMI WATTS IN 2002. THE
COUPLE REMAINED CLOSE FRIENDS AFTER THEIR BREAKUP
IN MAY 2004.

an impact the film would have on his career and
his life. Ledger was fresh from his breakup with
Naomi Watts when he started filming *Brokeback
Mountain.* The woman who played his wife,
Alma, was the former *Dawson's Creek* actress
Michelle Williams. In the film, Ledger's character
has a hard time developing feelings for Williams's
character. But in real life, the two formed an
almost immediate connection.

On the first day of shooting, Ledger and
Williams were filming a scene in which they

sledded down a snowy hill and fell off the sled. When Michelle started screaming in pain, Ledger thought she was acting. He soon realized that she had actually twisted her knee and was in great pain. Ledger insisted on going with her to the hospital. It was the first sign to the rest of the cast and crew that Ledger and Williams were more than just costars.

The couple grew closer. Eventually, they bought a home in Brooklyn, New York. Ledger seemed to be more grounded with Williams than he had been in past relationships. The two enjoyed cooking together, and they were often seen doing errands such as shopping in the local supermarket and using the laundromat. "She's my soul mate and we couldn't love each other any more than we do already. We're like two peas in a pod," Ledger said at the time.[2] They were about to become three peas in a pod.

## FATHERHOOD

By the time Ledger began working on his next movie, *Candy*, Williams was pregnant

### Older Women

It is no secret that Ledger was attracted to older women. His *Roar* costar Lisa Zane was 18 years older than he was. Actress Heather Graham was nine years older, and Naomi Watts ten years. "I prefer to date older women because they don't try to act older like younger girls, but because they try to act younger," Heath explained.[3] Ironically, the woman Ledger had described as his "soul mate," Michelle Williams, was two years younger than he was.

▲ MICHELLE WILLIAMS WITH LEDGER IN A SCENE FROM *BROKEBACK MOUNTAIN*

with their daughter. Matilda Rose was born on October 28, 2005. Williams chose the name *Matilda* because she loves the Roald Dahl book of the same name.

After Matilda's birth, Ledger took a few months off from acting to be with his family. It was just the three of them—Ledger, Williams, and Matilda—without family, friends, or even a nanny to help out. Every morning, Ledger was up by 6:00 a.m. to cook breakfast for Williams.

He watched Matilda when Williams had to work. Ledger was absolutely enamored with his baby, calling her, "this brilliant little person who's so full of life and so smart and happy."[4] Their Brooklyn neighbors often spotted Ledger carrying his young daughter on his shoulders, playing with her in the park, or taking her out for ice cream.

## SETTLING DOWN

Awards season made Ledger and Williams's relationship difficult for a few months, but they stuck together through it. Soon, they seemed to be settling into domestic bliss. In 2006, they bought a Hollywood home to use when they traveled to the West Coast. By November of that year, Ledger and Williams appeared to be discussing marriage. The press reported that they had applied for a marriage license in Brooklyn and were planning a January wedding. Reportedly, the two were spotted wearing wedding rings. They did not confirm or deny the rumors.

## THE BREAKUP

Despite Williams and Ledger's deep love for one another, by early 2007, their relationship was starting to fall apart. Ledger had some problems with illegal drugs and alcohol in the past.

Some people speculated that his partying and drug use had increased and were causing a rift between the two. Others said the couple's relationship was strained because they were often separated by their work. In March of that year, Williams was in New York during Fashion Week. Meanwhile, Ledger was spotted in a Los Angeles nightclub, allegedly surrounded by women.

After three years together, Ledger and Williams called it quits in September 2007 while Ledger was shooting *The Dark Knight.* Ledger was reportedly very upset about the breakup. He moved into an apartment at 421 Broome Street in New York's SoHo neighborhood. Williams stayed in their Brooklyn brownstone with Matilda, who was only two years old at the time. Despite the split, Ledger vowed to spend as much time with his daughter as possible. He set up a bedroom in his apartment for her visits.

## Tattoos

Ledger had several tattoos, including a dragonfly on his upper-right arm and "KAOS" around one wrist to represent his sisters' and mother's first initials. While he was dating Williams, he had the words "Old Man River" tattooed on his forearm. He said it had nothing to do with the song from the musical *Showboat.* In an interview, he explained, "I just felt there was something eternal about the phrase and I feel that I'm at a stage in my life now where life is just about to really speed up and flash by and so I feel like I am on old man river paddling on a little rowboat."[5]

## LIFE AFTER MICHELLE

Although Ledger was still reeling from his breakup with Michelle Williams, he did not waste time getting back into the dating scene. He was linked to a string of beautiful women, including model Helena Christensen and actresses Lindsay Lohan, Mary-Kate Olsen, and Kate Hudson. He also was seen with his former girlfriend Heather Graham.

By the end of 2007, and still only a few months after Ledger's split from Williams, the media reported that he was dating

### The Paparazzi

Celebrities have to get accustomed to being followed around by photographers and losing their privacy. At first, Ledger tried to find humor in the fact that the press was reporting everything about him. They even followed him on vacation in Mexico and took photos of him from a fishing boat. He tried to ignore them, but after a while, they started to annoy him.

Ledger became so tired of being stalked by the paparazzi that he fired back. While filming the movie *Candy* in Newtown, a suburb of Sydney, Australia, Ledger reportedly chased photographer Guy Finlay after Finlay snapped a photo of him. Finlay claimed to have suffered a sore elbow and calf muscle from the incident.

The photographer got his revenge in 2006. As Ledger and girlfriend Michelle Williams walked down the red carpet at the Australian premiere of *Brokeback Mountain* in Sydney, a group of paparazzi led by Finlay opened fire with water pistols. Ledger was soaked and had to introduce his movie while soaking wet. Two months later, he and Williams sold their Sydney home, claiming they were tired of dealing with the intrusive Australian photographers.

▲ WILLIAMS WITH DAUGHTER MATILDA IN 2009

Gemma Ward, a 21-year-old Australian model. They were seen together in Australia when he returned home to visit family over the Christmas holiday. Ward would be Ledger's last relationship.

# 8

# FINAL ROLES

*T*aking on the role of the legendary Italian lover Casanova was a complete switch for Ledger after playing the emotionally repressed Ennis Del Mar in *Brokeback Mountain.* The historical Casanova was so charming and so in love with women that his name became synonymous with romance. In the movie, Casanova meets the first woman in his life (Francesca, played by Sienna Miller) who can resist his charms and falls completely in love with her.

Ledger loved the script, and he admired director Lasse Hallström, who had previously worked on such films as *The Cider House Rules* and *Chocolat*. This time, Ledger would be playing a real person (unlike Ennis Del Mar, who was a fictional character). Though Ledger carefully researched Casanova's life, he also wanted to give the character his own spin.

The film was shot in Venice, Italy, over four and a half months in 2004. Ledger loved the city—its wine, pasta, and gondolas. This film shoot was much more laid-back than the physically and mentally exhausting *Brokeback Mountain* shoot that he had just finished.

## CANDY

After the success of *Brokeback Mountain*, film roles came quickly to Ledger. His next film after *Casanova* was *Candy*, a low-budget Australian movie about a young couple who become addicted to the illegal drug heroin. The movie was based on the 1997 novel of the same name by author Luke Davies. It was Davies who recommended Ledger for the part of Dan, the poet who falls in love with a beautiful

"I don't want to do this for the rest of my life . . . . I don't want to spend the rest of my youth doing this in this industry. There's so much I want to discover."[1]

—Heath Ledger, 2000

painter named Candy, played by Abbie Cornish.

To film *Candy,* Ledger returned to Australia. He was relieved that he did not have to adopt a foreign accent, as he had in several of his previous roles. The character did require a lot of preparation, though. Both Ledger and Cornish spent time at a rehabilitation center to learn how people abuse drugs.

*Candy* was released in 2006. Though critics loved Ledger's performance in the film, it was an art movie and not a blockbuster. As a result, *Candy* did not receive much attention in the United States.

## I'M NOT THERE

Ledger's next movie was also not blockbuster material. It was a quirky, original film by director Todd Haynes called *I'm Not There*. In it, Ledger played one of six characters. Each character represents a different stage in the life and music of Bob Dylan. Christian Bale, Richard Gere, and even one female actor, Cate Blanchett, all played versions of the music icon.

**Insecurity**

No matter how many awards Ledger won and how many of his peers praised his acting ability, he was never fully confident about his talent. "I always want to pull myself apart and dissect it," he said. "I go through the process of hating it, hating myself, thinking I've fooled them, I can't actually do this."[2]

▲ LEDGER PLAYED GUITAR AS ROBBIE CLARK IN *I'M NOT THERE*. THE ROLE LED TO LEDGER'S OBSESSION WITH BOB DYLAN'S MUSIC.

Ledger's character, Robbie Clark, represented Bob Dylan as an actor and celebrity. Once again, Ledger spent a lot of time preparing for the role. He read books, watched documentaries, and listened to Dylan's music to get inside his character. Ledger said he was already a fan of Dylan's music when he got the role. However, landing the part led to an obsession with the musician.

## THE JOKER

Ledger also became obsessed with his next character, the Joker, producing one of the greatest acting performances of his career. While Ledger was becoming famous and film offers began to come his way, he vowed that he would never play a superhero on screen. Wearing tights and acting heroic just did not appeal to him. So when director Christopher Nolan discussed casting Ledger in the title role in his 2005 film *Batman Begins,* Ledger turned him down. Christian Bale, Ledger's costar from *I'm Not There*, took the role of Batman instead. Yet when Nolan came calling again a few years later with a part in the sequel, *The Dark Knight*, Ledger reconsidered.

> "Music, on so many levels, has affected my life and still continues to. . . . It's always been a key that unlocked or enabled me to express anger or pains of any sort."[3]
> —*Heath Ledger, in an interview for* I'm Not There

This time, the part was not playing a superhero, but a super villain. Cesar Romero and Jack Nicholson had each played the Joker on screen. Romero starred in the 1960s *Batman* television series, and Nicholson took on the role in the 1989 Tim Burton movie. Both actors had given the character a comical spin, but Ledger's Joker was meant to be darker and more sinister.

Ledger always spent time preparing for his roles—this one in particular. He started to gather ideas for the Joker's character months before the shoot began. He sat in a hotel room for weeks, experimenting with different voices until he found the one that perfectly captured the Joker's diabolical nature.

Ledger told reporters that his role in *The Dark Knight* was his favorite. He loved playing the evil and out-of-control character. Theatergoers also loved Ledger's interpretation of the Joker. When *The Dark Knight* was released on July 18, 2008, it made $158 million in its opening weekend. Eventually, the film earned more than $1 billion worldwide, making it the second-highest-grossing film in U.S. movie history.

Many critics said Ledger's performance was behind the movie's success. "This is a career-making performance if

## The Joker

Heath Ledger transformed himself for the part of the Joker in *The Dark Knight*. That change went far deeper than the smudged white makeup and smeared, blood-red lips. He inhabited the psychopathic killer.

Many people have speculated that playing the role contributed to Ledger's untimely death. They believe he became so wrapped up in the dark character that he could not sleep and started taking the dangerous mix of prescription medications that ultimately killed him.

Actor Jack Nicholson, who had portrayed the character in a 1989 movie, told reporters that he had warned Ledger about taking the part. Although Nicholson was not clear exactly what he had meant by the warning, it is possible that he also was deeply affected by playing the character.

▲ Ledger's darkest role was the Joker in *The Dark Knight*.

ever there was one," wrote a reporter from *USA Today*.[4] "His haunting Joker helps make *The Dark Knight* unforgettable," another reviewer wrote.[5]

## DOCTOR PARNASSUS

In late 2007, Ledger had barely finished *The Dark Knight* when he was offered his next role, a part in *The Imaginarium of Doctor Parnassus*. Once again, Ledger teamed up with Terry Gilliam, who had directed him in *The Brothers Grimm*. Gilliam had cowritten the script for *The Imaginarium of Doctor Parnassus* with British writer Charles McKeown. The story was about an ancient magician, Doctor Parnassus, who was played by Christopher Plummer. Parnassus makes a deal with the devil that allows his audiences to travel through a magical mirror into a fantasy world where they can live out their dreams. In exchange, Parnassus must provide the devil with five souls—or give up his daughter in exchange. When Tony, played by Ledger, joins the magic troupe, he has to help save the daughter from the devil.

▲ LEDGER'S LAST ROLE WAS TONY IN *THE IMAGINARIUM OF DOCTOR PARNASSUS*.

Shooting on the movie was scheduled to begin in November 2007, but Ledger was still filming *The Dark Knight*. Gilliam waited until early December to accommodate Ledger's schedule. When Ledger arrived, practically straight from the other movie set, he was still emotionally wrapped up in the Joker. He was exhausted, stressed, and still getting over his breakup with Michelle Williams. It was a dark and difficult time for the 28-year-old actor.

———•◆•———

# 9

# TRAGIC DEATH

edger was working nonstop. He had just finished filming the emotionally draining role of the Joker in *The Dark Knight* when he traveled to London to start shooting *The Imaginarium of Doctor Parnassus.* For a while, he was flying back and forth between London and New York.

Meanwhile, Ledger was in the middle of a nasty custody dispute with his former girlfriend, Michelle Williams, over their two-year-old daughter, Matilda. Ledger was reportedly afraid that he would not get to see his daughter as much

▶ PLAYING THE JOKER WAS EMOTIONALLY DRAINING FOR LEDGER.

as he wanted. He loved Matilda deeply and could not bear to be away from her for long.

The stress of work and the anxiety over his failed relationship were keeping Ledger up at night. By the end of filming *The Dark Knight,* he said he was sleeping about two hours a night. He started taking prescription sleep medications to help him get some rest.

In addition, while shooting *Doctor Parnassus,* Ledger came down with pneumonia. When he showed up on the set sick, the doctor told him to go home. Ledger refused. His work kept him going, even while he was sick. "By the end of the day he was beaming, glowing with energy," said Gilliam. "It was like everything was put into the work, because that was the joy; that's what he loved to do."[1]

The London portion of the *Doctor Parnassus* shoot

## One Actor Becomes Three

When Ledger died, many of his scenes in *The Imaginarium of Doctor Parnassus* were still unfinished. Initially, director Terry Gilliam wanted to stop production. But with millions of dollars at stake, he came up with a creative way to complete the movie. He called in three actors, Johnny Depp, Jude Law, and Colin Farrell, to take over for Ledger. Because their scenes were shot on the other side of the mirror in a fantasy world, it was somewhat easy to get away with the switch. The triple performance became a kind of tribute to Ledger. When the movie premiered at the Cannes Film Festival in France on May 22, 2009, audiences gave it a ten-minute standing ovation. *The Imaginarium of Doctor Parnassus* was dedicated to Ledger and to producer William Vince, who died after the movie wrapped.

wrapped on January 19, 2008. Ledger decided to return to New York for a week to rest and recover. He was also planning to meet with director Steven Spielberg to discuss a role in an upcoming movie about the Chicago Seven, a group of seven men who were arrested for their role in protesting at the 1968 Democratic National Convention in Chicago. On January 20, Ledger boarded a flight to New York.

## JANUARY 22, 2008

On Tuesday, January 22, Ledger's housekeeper, Teresa Solomon, came to clean his apartment, just as she did every Tuesday. She let herself in with a key and saw a note on the refrigerator in Ledger's handwriting that he had a 3:00 p.m. massage appointment. When Solomon went into Ledger's bedroom at around 1:00 p.m., she found him fast asleep.

At 2:45 p.m., massage therapist Diana Wolozin arrived. Neither she nor Solomon wanted to wake Ledger. They figured they would let him sleep for a few more minutes. When he still had not come out of his bedroom 25 minutes later, Wolozin called Ledger on his cell phone to wake him. He did not answer. Then she knocked on his bedroom door. Finally, she let herself into his room to set up her table for the massage.

When she tried to shake him, he was cold and did not respond.

Instead of calling 9-1-1 for help, Wolozin used Ledger's cell phone to dial his friend, actress Mary-Kate Olsen. Wolozin claimed she did not want to alert media attention, but the call still remains controversial. At the time, Olsen was in her manager's office in Beverly Hills, California, so she sent for her private security guards. Wolozin called Olsen three times before finally calling 9-1-1 at 3:26 p.m. At just after 3:30 p.m., New York Fire Department paramedics and Olsen's security guards arrived at Ledger's apartment. The paramedics tried to perform CPR, but it was too late. The 28-year-old Heath Ledger was dead.

### WHY DID LEDGER DIE?

Police soon found the culprit in Ledger's death—a mixture of six different prescription medications that he was using to relieve pain, ease anxiety, and get to sleep. Each of the drugs was legal and safe when used individually. But the mixture of all six medications proved deadly. The question was whether Ledger had taken the drugs on purpose. Had he been trying to harm himself?

Ledger was no stranger to drugs and alcohol. Many reports stated that it was his drinking

▲ FANS AND FRIENDS LEFT FLOWERS AND PHOTOS
IN MEMORIAL TO LEDGER OUTSIDE HIS NEW YORK
APARTMENT.

and drug use that had led to his breakup with
Michelle Williams. In March 2006, Williams
reportedly drove Ledger to Promises Treatment
Center, a drug rehabilitation facility in Malibu,
California. Ledger had refused to check in, but
he admitted that he needed to stop what he was
doing.

After a thorough investigation, the New York
City medical examiner's office ruled Ledger's
death an accident. They believed he had been

seeing several different doctors in the United States and Europe who had prescribed the drugs. The doctors may not have realized that Ledger was taking all the medications at the same time.

## FANS MOURN

In a world of 24-hour news channels, word of a celebrity's death travels quickly—especially when that celebrity is young and popular. Within hours of Ledger's death, camera crews and hundreds of fans had gathered outside his SoHo apartment building. They left makeshift memorials of flowers and notes. One note read, "Yesterday you were a star, today you are a legend for New York. Thank you for being a member of the Brooklyn family."[2]

The news spread so quickly

### Unfinished Business

When Ledger died, he was in the middle of filming *The Imaginarium of Doctor Parnassus*. Ledger was not the first actor to die while filming a movie. In 1993, Brandon Lee, son of martial arts star Bruce Lee, died in an accident on the set of *The Crow*. At first, producers were not sure whether to finish the movie. Ultimately, stunt doubles and computer animation were used to complete Lee's scenes. When River Phoenix died of a drug overdose in 1993, he was almost done filming *Dark Blood*. However, because producers could not shoot the final scenes without him, the movie was never released.

Other actors who died before their movies were finished include Natalie Wood (died in 1981 while filming *Brainstorm*), Jean Harlow (died in 1937 while filming *Saratoga*), and that many of Ledger's family members found out about his death from television coverage. Williams was told about Ledger while she was shooting a movie in Sweden. Matilda was with her. Friends said Williams was absolutely devastated by the news. She and Matilda returned to Brooklyn on Wednesday, January 23—the day after Ledger's death.

## CELEBRITY MEMORIALS

While Ledger's fans mourned his loss publicly, those who knew him well gathered to say their goodbyes to the man they had loved so dearly. Friends and family members held a private memorial at Pierce Brothers Mortuary in Los Angeles on January 26. It was the first of several remembrances of Ledger's life.

On February 2, Tom Cruise, his wife Katie Holmes (Williams's former *Dawson's Creek* costar), Sienna Miller, Ellen DeGeneres, Gemma Ward, Naomi Watts, Orlando Bloom, and other celebrities held a 90-minute tribute to Ledger on the Sony Studios lot in Culver City, California. Todd Haynes, director of *I'm Not There*, spoke about Ledger. Ben Harper sang.

Ledger's body was brought home to Perth, Australia, on February 5. Four days later, approximately 500 friends and family members attended a memorial service at Penrhos College, a private girls' school in the Perth suburb of Como. Ledger's parents, sister Kate, and actress Cate Blanchett read moving tributes to Ledger.

After the ceremony, close family and friends went to Fremantle Cemetery for a service. Ledger's ashes were scattered in a family plot at Karrakatta Cemetery, where two of his grandparents are buried. Williams read Shakespeare's "Sonnet 18," which begins, "Shall I compare thee to a summer's day?"

The service was followed by a wake at the Indiana Tea House, a beautiful restaurant on Cottesloe Beach along the Indian Ocean. It had been one of Ledger's favorite surfing spots. Some of the guests walked to the water's edge, slipped off their shoes, and danced to remember Ledger. Williams, who had spent much of the day hiding her tears behind dark glasses, was reluctant to join them. Eventually, she got in the water too, and her spirits brightened.

"To most of the world Heath was an actor of immeasurable talent and promise. To those who knew him personally, Heath was a consummate artist whose passions also included photography, music, chess, and directing. We knew Heath as a loving father, as our devoted son, and as a loyal and generous brother and friend."[3]
—Ledger family statement

## POSTHUMOUS HONORS
When *The Dark Knight* was released in summer 2008,

▲ WILLIAMS, *WEARING WHITE DRESS*, DANCES ON THE BEACH IN CELEBRATION OF LEDGER AT HIS MEMORIAL.

Hollywood began buzzing about the awards Ledger might receive for the Joker. On Ledger's behalf, director Christopher Nolan accepted a Golden Globe Award for Best Performance by an Actor in a Supporting Role in a Motion Picture and Gary Oldman accepted the Screen Actors Guild Award for Outstanding Performance by a Male Actor in a Supporting Role.

On January 22, 2009, the first anniversary of his death, Ledger was nominated for an Academy Award for Best Supporting Actor.

▲ A TRIBUTE TO LEDGER RAN AT THE CRITIC'S CHOICE
AWARDS. DIRECTOR CHRISTOPHER NOLAN ACCEPTED
LEDGER'S AWARD FOR BEST SUPPORTING ACTOR.

A month later, his family was at the Kodak
Theater in Los Angeles to accept that award.
His father said, "This award tonight would have
humbly validated Heath's quiet determination to
be truly accepted by you all here, his peers within
an industry he so loved."[4]

## LIFE AFTER HEATH LEDGER
Months after his untimely death, Ledger's family
and friends were still healing from the loss.

Williams continued to raise their daughter Matilda in the Brooklyn town house where they had briefly lived together as a family. Meanwhile, his family remembered the "down-to-earth, generous, kindhearted" man they knew.[5] And his fans watched and rewatched his movies.

Ledger's family, friends, and fans will always mourn the loss of a talent taken far too young and a career that was full of so much promise. Yet in many ways, Ledger was far older than his 28 years when he died, and he felt a sort of contentment that many people do not achieve until far later in life. In an interview given the November before his death, Ledger said something about his daughter that now seems eerie, as if Ledger had foretold his own death. "I feel good about dying now, because I feel like I'm alive in her, but at the same time, you don't want to die because you want to be around for the rest of her life."[6] In a way, Ledger does live on—in his films and in the little girl who looks so much like her father.

| **1979** | **1996** | **1997** |
|---|---|---|
| Heath Ledger is born on April 4 in Perth, Australia. | Ledger's first episode of the Australian television show *Sweat* airs. | Ledger makes his film debut in *Blackrock*. |

| **2001** | **2002** | **2003** |
|---|---|---|
| *A Knight's Tale* debuts with the slogan "He will rock you." | Ledger costars with Halle Berry and Billy Bob Thornton in *Monster's Ball*. | Ledger portrays a priest investigating a mystery in *The Order*. |

## 1999

*10 Things I Hate About You*, Ledger's U.S. film debut, is released.

## 1999

Ledger stars in the Australian film *Two Hands*.

## 2000

*The Patriot,* starring Mel Gibson and Ledger, is released.

## 2004

Ledger stars in the Australian film *Ned Kelly*.

## 2005

Three of Ledger's movies—*Brokeback Mountain*, *The Brothers Grimm*, and *Casanova*—premiere at the Venice Film Festival.

## 2005

Daughter Matilda Rose is born to Heath Ledger and girlfriend Michelle Williams on October 28.

#  TIMELINE

## 2005

*Brokeback Mountain*, the turning point in Ledger's film career, is released on December 16.

## 2007

On September 4, Michelle Williams's father, Larry, confirms that his daughter and Ledger have broken up.

## 2008

The London portion of *The Imaginarium of Doctor Parnassus* finishes shooting on January 19.

## 2008

On February 2, celebrities hold a tribute to Ledger on the Sony Studios lot in Culver City, California.

## 2008

On February 9, friends and family attend a memorial service in Perth, Australia, followed by a wake at Cottesloe Beach.

## 2008

*The Dark Knight* is released to rave reviews on July 18.

## 2008

Ledger returns to New York on January 20 for a break from filming.

## 2008

On January 22, Ledger is found dead in his New York apartment of an apparent drug overdose.

## 2008

Friends and family hold a private memorial for Ledger in Los Angeles on January 26.

## 2009

On January 22, the first anniversary of Ledger's death, he is nominated for an Academy Award for *The Dark Knight*.

## 2009

On February 22, Ledger wins the Best Supporting Actor Oscar for *The Dark Knight*.

## 2009

*Doctor Parnassus* premieres at the Cannes Film Festival on May 22. Audiences give it a ten-minute standing ovation.

# QUICK FACTS

**DATE OF BIRTH**
April 4, 1979

**PLACE OF BIRTH**
Perth, Australia

**DATE OF DEATH**
January 22, 2008

**PLACE OF DEATH**
Manhattan, New York

**PARENTS**
Sally Bell and Kim Ledger

**CHILDREN**
Matilda Rose (with Michelle Williams)

**CAREER HIGHLIGHTS**

**Television**
*Ship to Shore* (1993)
*Sweat* (1996)
*Bush Patrol* (ca. 1997)
*Corrigan* (ca. 1997)
*Home and Away* (1997)
*Roar* (1997)

**Movies**
*Clowning Around* (1991)
*Blackrock* (1997)
*Paws* (1997)
*10 Things I Hate About You* (1999)
*The Patriot* (2000)
*A Knight's Tale* (2001)
*Monster's Ball* (2001)
*The Four Feathers* (2002)
*The Order* (2003)
*Ned Kelly* (2003)
*Lords of Dogtown* (2005)
*The Brothers Grimm* (2005)
*Brokeback Mountain* (2005)
*Casanova* (2005)
*Candy* (2006)
*I'm Not There* (2007)
*The Dark Knight* (2008)
*The Imaginarium of Doctor Parnassus* (2009)

## QUOTE

"The only time that I'm alive and loving and expressing and feeling and relating is when I'm on set during the time between 'action' and 'cut.' That's the only thing that's really important."—*Heath Ledger*

# ADDITIONAL RESOURCES

## SELECT BIBLIOGRAPHY

"Actor Heath Ledger Remembered." *ABC News*. 23 Jan. 2008.
<http://abcnews.go.com/print?id=4175704>.

Bernstein, Adam, and David Segal. "A Star's Bright, Brief
Life." *Washingtonpost.com*. 23 Jan. 2008. <http://www.
washingtonpost.com/wp-dyn/content/article/2008/01/22/
AR2008012202352.html>.

"Heath Ledger: Biography." *Variety*. <www.variety.com/profiles/
people/Biography/28390/Heath+Ledger.html?dataSet=1>.

Lipsky, David. "1979–2008: Heath Ledger." *Rolling Stone*. 21
Feb. 2008.

Robb, Brian J. *Heath Ledger: Hollywood's Dark Star*. London,
Eng.: Plexus Publishing Limited, 2008.

## FURTHER READING

Anderson, Wendy. *Livewire Real Lives: Heath Ledger*.
Cambridge, Eng.: Cambridge University Press, 2003.

Bankston, John. *Heath Ledger (Galaxy of Superstars)*. New York,
NY: Chelsea House Publications, 2002.

Krulik, Nancy. *The Heath Is On!* New York, NY: Simon &
Schuster, 2001.

## WEB LINKS

To learn more about Heath Ledger, visit ABDO Publishing Company online at **www.abdopublishing.com**. Web sites about Heath Ledger are featured on our Book Links page. These links are routinely monitored and updated to provide the most current information available.

## FOR MORE INFORMATION

For more information on this subject, contact or visit the following organizations.

### Australians in Film, Heath Ledger Scholarship
www.aifhls.com
The organization Australians in Film presents an annual scholarship in Heath Ledger's honor to aspiring Australian actors. The scholarship allows them to travel to the United States or other countries to improve their craft and further their careers.

### City of Perth, Australia
www.cityofperth.wa.gov.au
Tourists interested in visiting Heath Ledger's hometown of Perth, Australia, can learn more about the area through the city's official Web site.

# LOSSARY

**camaraderie**
A friendship or easy relationship between two or more people.

**Celtic**
A term used to describe people who spoke the Celtic language in Great Britain and Ireland.

**cinematographer**
The person who does the filming of a movie and gives it the desired look.

**controversial**
Causing debate among people with different viewpoints.

**franchise**
A series of movies based on the same story and characters.

**improvisation**
Making something up (such as a play or comedy skit) as a person goes along, rather than reading from a script.

**intrusive**
Something or someone that is not welcome.

**jousting**
An ancient sport in which two knights on horseback fight each other with long, pointed rods called lances.

**legacy**
Something that a person leaves behind when he or she dies.

## Chapter 8. Final Roles

1. "Biography for Heath Ledger." *IMDb*. 9 July 2009 <http://www.imdb.com/name/nm0005132/bio>.
2. David Lipsky. "1979–2008: Heath Ledger." *Rolling Stone* 21 Feb. 2008: 35.
3. Max Evry. "Interview: Heath Ledger on 'I'm Not There.'" *Cinecon.com*. 22 Nov. 2007. 27 July 2009 <http://www.cinecon.com/news/1125/interview-heath-ledger-im-not-there/>.
4. Claudia Puig. "Ledger's Talent Lives on As The Joker In 'Dark Knight.'" *USA Today*. 1 Aug. 2008. 27 July 2009 <http://www.usatoday.com/life/movies/reviews/2008-07-16-dark-knight-review_N.htm>.
5. Jason Lynch. "PEOPLE Review: No Joke—Heath Ledger Makes *The Dark Knight* Unforgettable." *People*. 16 July 2008. 27 July 2009 <http://www.people.com/people/article/0,,20212604,00.html>.


## Chapter 9. Tragic Death

1. Peter Biskind. "The Last of Heath." *Vanity Fair* Aug. 2009: 132.
2. Nicole Sperling. "Heath Ledger: The Mourning After." *Entertainment Weekly* 8 Feb. 2008: 12.
3. "Text of Statement by Heath Ledger's Family." *AAP General News Wire*. 6 Feb. 2008. 1.
4. "Heath's Family Accepts Oscar for Matilda." *Star Magazine*. 23 Feb. 2009. 28 July 2009 <http://www.starmagazine.com/news/15266>.
5. "Actor Heath Ledger Remembered." *ABC News*. 23 Jan. 2008. 8 July 2009 <http://abcnews.go.com/print?id=4175704>.
6. Ibid.
7. Peter Biskind. "The Last of Heath." *Vanity Fair* Aug. 2009: 136.

# INDEX

# ABOUT THE AUTHOR

Stephanie Watson is a freelance writer based in Atlanta, Georgia. She writes for a variety of publications and has penned nearly two dozen books on subjects ranging from fast food to recycling. Titles include *Anderson Cooper: Profile of a TV Journalist*, *Sports Families: The Earnhardt NASCAR Dynasty*, *Daniel Radcliffe*, and *This Is Me: Facing Physical Challenges*.

# PHOTO CREDITS